Tuba

HYMNS FOR BRASS

arranged for brass quintet
by Rick Walters

easy level

THE CANADIAN BRASS

CANADIAN
BRASS
SERIES OF
COLLECTED QUINTETS

Ah, Holy Jesus

TUBA

Johannes Crüger
("Herzliebster Jesu")

Christ the Lord is Risen Today

TUBA

from *Lyra Davidica,* 1708

Eternal Father, Strong to Save

TUBA

John B. Dykes, c. 1861

Beautiful Savior

TUBA

Silesian Melody
(Schönster Herr Jesu)

A Mighty Fortress

TUBA

Martin Luther, 1529

We Gather Together

TUBA

Netherlands Folk Song, 1626

C A N A D I A N
B R A S S
SERIES OF
COLLECTED QUINTETS

HYMNS FOR BRASS

arranged for brass quintet
by Rick Walters

contents

2 Ah, Holy Jesus (Johannes Crüger)

3 Christ the Lord is Risen Today
(from *Lyra Davidica*)

4 Eternal Father, Strong to Save (John B. Dykes)

5 Beautiful Savior (Silesian Melody)

6 A Mighty Fortress (Martin Luther)

7 We Gather Together
(Netherlands Folk Song)

Welcome to the new *Canadian Brass Series of Collected Quintets*. In our work with students we have for some time been aware of the need for more brass quintet music at easy and intermediate levels of difficulty. We are continually observing a kind of "Renaissance" in brass music, not only in audience responses to our quintet, but to all brass music in general. The brass quintet, as a chamber ensemble, seems to have become as standard a chamber combination as a string quartet. That could not have been said twenty-five years ago. Brass quintets are popping up everywhere — professional quintets, junior and senior high school ensembles, college and university groups, and amateur quintets of adult players.

We have carefully chosen the literature for these collected quintets, and closely supervised the arrangements. Our aim was to retain a Canadian Brass flavor to each arrangement, and create attractive repertory designed so that any brass quintet can play it with satisfying results. We've often remarked to one another that we certainly wish that we'd had quintet arrangements like these when we were students!

Happy playing to you and your quintet.

— THE CANADIAN BRASS

U.S. $9.99

0 73999 88758 7

HL50488758

HAL•LEONARD®
CORPORATION
7777 W. BLUEMOUND RD. P.O. BOX 13819 MILWAUKEE, WI 53213